Otherwise, we are safe

poems by

OLIVIA STIFFLER

DOS MADRES PRESS INC.

P.O.Box 294, Loveland, Ohio 45140

www.dosmadres.com   editor@dosmadres.com

Dos Madres is dedicated to the belief that the small press is essential to the vitality of contemporary literature as a carrier of the new voice, as well as the older, sometimes forgotten voices of the past. And in an ever more virtual world, to the creation of fine books pleasing to the eye and hand.

Dos Madres is named in honor of Vera Murphy and Libbie Hughes, the "Dos Madres" whose contributions have made this press possible.

Dos Madres Press, Inc. is an Ohio Not For Profit Corporation and a 501 (c) (3) qualified public charity. Contributions are tax deductible.

Executive Editor: Robert J. Murphy

Illustration & Book Design: Elizabeth H. Murphy
www.illusionstudios.net

Typset in Adobe Garamond Pro & Angostura
ISBN 978-1-939929-00-6
Library of Congress Control Number: 2013940124

First Edition

DEDICATED

to poet and teacher James E. Tolan, without whom these poems would be asleep in a notebook without a title

to the publishers for their abundance of faith

to Avery, Shannon, and Al, my comfort and my strength

and to the memory of my mom, Josephine Ruth Edna Cheff Schwach, 1926-2005, the first love of my life.

TABLE OF CONTENTS

I

II

III

IV

I

SHELTER

My brother bends one at a time
the stand of lean saplings into a shelter
in the forest where we play. He works hard,
roofing with sod he carves from a grassy place
beyond the trees. With a piece of discarded lumber
he scrapes the dirt floor until it favors the brown-glass
beer bottles we find on the highway, load into our wagon,
and redeem for 2 cents each at the only store in town.

I work too:
       sweeping with a tree-branch broom
       foraging for the right leaves
       for pretend food, and the right twigs
       for forks, and the right rocks for chairs.

Not once during our busy day
does my brother raise his voice to me,
though our father's words hammering our mother
must echo in his head. We sit in our playhouse at the lip
of Hubble Creek like a quiet old couple, our shared secrets
not even a whisper between us, unconcerned about our neighbors,
the copperheads and cottonmouths that hide in their own dark places.

At our real home a thick black belt
coils around our father's waist,
ready with its hiss and bite and sting.
And though the red of evening
starts a slow burn in our empty bellies,
we are in no hurry to get back there.

A QUESTION OF SEASONS

We sit side by side on the sofa.
"I thought we would grow old
together," I say. "So did I,"
my mother replies, "So did I."
"When?" I ask because I'm sure
she knows. "In the spring," she says.

We no longer shepherd our words.
That was for yesterday,
so full of tomorrows we could afford
to jockey lies. Time has turned on us.
It slides like hourglass sand
through the mouth of a slick funnel.

Behind thick glasses her near-blind eyes
search the perimeter, then draw a bead
on wallpaper birds. But when she fires:
"What if there is nothing else?"
I am the one gut-shot. It is the eleventh hour,
and I fall hard into her Gethsemane, my tongue
teetering like a seesaw between a symphony
of lies and the chorus of my disbelief.
Words hide. Time hangs a noose above my head.
To avoid being her Judas, I would bargain
with anybody's devil from anybody's hell.

Cushioned in her stillness, she waits
for my answer, and the words I finally blurt
prick like a splinter nagging flesh.
"If there is nothing, you won't know."
Looking straight ahead, she leans
forward and reaches for her rolling legs.
"I think I'll rest awhile."

We inch down the darkening hallway,
silence gathering on us like dust,
toward her rumpled home hospital-bed.
Outside on the birdhouse roofs
the last clumps of winter-weary snow
are melting into teardrops.

LAST RITES

ABSOLUTION

She stares at the chart so long she could be reading
the future in tea leaves instead of solemn black numbers.
No surprises here. Like a lion trainer she controlled
her old enemy, fed an arsenal of chemicals down
its long throat, whipped its tail between its legs.
But her bag of tricks is empty, and the beast is back,
refreshed and hungry. Today she lays down the lash
and accepts defeat. Buying time to subdue the shame
building in her belly like sickness, she stretches a note
across the bone-white paper, pen heavy as an ax, ego
stewing that she is not God, not God, not God. And she
forgives herself the loss of this person who is slipping
through her fingers like a rosary bead. Time to get it
over with. Her hands fold into a miniature church,
pressed indexes the steeple, crossed thumbs the door.
As she tilts backward, her squeaking chair defiles
the silence like screaming in a cloister. Then she intones
the last rites of oncology over my mother's wasting body:
                    "There is nothing more we can do for you."

ANOINTING

This time, she did not hem her own dress. No matter.
It gathers in her wheelchair in restless waves
of spilled honey as she searches for her granddaughter
in the opaque cloud of wedding white at the altar.
Conveyed like a queen in a litter by an honor guard
of relatives, she seems to float through the rituals
as familiar guests gather around her like children
at story time. Shy at first, they linger in the spell
of her quivering life-- thin and luminous as the gold
threads spinning through her gown--and inhale
the perfume that sighs from her like ebbing roses
breathing into darkness. Not as late as midnight,

4

but for a while she glistens, then folds into sleep,
weightless as a butterfly in the palm of God.
Breakfast marks the end of the celebration,
and the table has long been cleared. Now the dread
of leaving is a stone lying on her chest. As if to mock
this dark mood, the sun lifts its golden-monstrance
above a canvas of morning lawn, where her clan,
framed by the rear window of the hesitating car, spread
against the pale grass like the dots of an Impressionist
master. The growing distance between her and her people
racks her with pain, a burning worse than any horror
of the years of illness, and she chokes back a sob.
But needles of tears escape and shroud the receding specks
of her family as they turn to talk to each other,
unaware of the cost to her of this last sacrament,
the love that anoints them through the vanishing light.
VIATICUM
They cut her loose today. No more torture.
Back at the house, bought in the wake of her cancer
because it sat near the hospital like a guard shack
heralding a fortress, she stops at the threshold.
"You've been a good home," she says, addressing
the door like an old friend about to move
to a new country. One more time I help her inside
where she holds out her arms to be dressed
in the bed jacket bought for her birthday and tries
to eat the lobster. But nothing can anchor her.
She is an untied balloon lifting out of reach,
and before I realize she is going, she quiets
into an expanding universe of coma
while her night nurse and I share a bowl
of popcorn across the table of her body
like children at a slumber party. At three
in the morning I wake with my back

against metal bed rails. We are alone,
my mother and I, the way we started,
and so close I can taste the last breath
from the fish oval of her mouth
but not yet the bitterness
pooling in my cup
one drop
of grief
at a time.

WISTFUL THINKING

What if you lived in your own little house
near to mine across the bridge? I could
walk there in winter. We could sip hot
chocolate or tea and wrap ourselves in the
spongy fleece comforters my sisters bought
you for Christmas. In spring you'd name
your garden flowers and tell me how to care
for them, firm in your belief I need to know
though I have seldom taken spade to earth.
Just as I did long ago, I would lay my problems
out. They are few now, and not pressing, but
I would reveal them the way a child shows its
bruises, so you would see I still have hurts
for you to bandage. But I am only weaving a
shroud of hopeless dreams. There will be no
Lazarus-like miracles for us, not today, not ever.

MOCKERY

From her bed on the porch my mother watched
the hydrangea she planted the spring before flaunt
its fat, healthy globes of sapphire-blue. Showing off
like a rich kid in front of one who is poor, I thought.
Now I wonder if she hated that plant the way I did
or if she spent her last hours hating anything at all.

BENEDICTION AT ST. EDWARD'S

Fr. Schmidt moves a spoonful of gray dust
from a small silver cup to a fancy large one
with a pointed lid. He whispers over it,
swings it toward the altar from a chain that
lifts from three sides in a braided pyramid,
and turns to face us, whispering and swinging
until greenish smoke rolls out of the cup like
rain clouds and falls on old Mr. Probst, an
empty feedsack slumping in his worn gray
suit, the only soul in the front pew. A smell
of heavy spice soaks the air, creeps into my eyes
and nose and throat, and my child's mind
believes it rises—like the stench of steam when
water douses the breath from a smoldering fire—
not from any priestly magic but from the old man
himself.

ARMCHAIR KILLERS

We engineered their deaths coiled
on the concrete stoop of my house.
We would lure them into the woods.
We never said how or when.
We would shoot them.
We never said with what gun.
We would be free.
No more days stomped in the middle
like cans for the trash. No more
whore-slap-brat-spite-bitch-blame.
Yoked in the pure, hard logic
of children with nothing to lose,
day after day we plowed our grievances,
watered our plans, imagined the harvest.
Neither of us ever prosecuted for murder,
the intention not the same as the deed.
Sheila joined then left the convent.
I married and divorced the prince of lies.
Her mother died.
My father drools on his bib in the nursing home.
To this day I don't know if Sheila was serious.

LEARNING TO LIE

Of course, I did it,
wrote the word in orange crayon
on our new concrete porch.
Not like a kid who leaves a message
in a bottle, hoping someone will read it.
I did it
because I knew it would be beautiful.
I was sitting on that cold, clean canvas
when the devil whispered: "Want to see
how the letters look standing close together
like friends? The T will stretch out its arms
in the sign of the cross. The E will grow
fingers and the R's legs. Arms in the air,
the Y will surrender the name of your friend:
T-E-R-R-Y."

"Did you do that?" my father asks.
Yes? No? He will whip me either way.
So I just say no because, sin or not,
I plan to consult this devil again soon.

BROKEN

The hardwood floors in my sister's house
   buckle where he has peed on them.
His trembling hands release her china,
   and it shatters against the kitchen tile.
With a metal cane he bashes the heavy oak
   doors that resist his pushing and pulling.
Widowed and aging, our father rips and tears
   at his new nest, marks his territory, and exacts
   revenge against those who care for him.

TV soap operas consume his days and segue
   into personal dramas. Phantom "punk kids"
   get into the house despite the locks
   and leap out at him from closets. They grow
   bold and have sex on the downstairs sofa.
He challenges whoever does not believe
   in them and traps two in the furnace room
   that escape before my sister returns from work,
   and he is so angry he doesn't speak for days.

Home late, my sister finds him at the bottom
   of her basement stairs, head cracked
   like Humpty-Dumpty, a mix of blood
   and memories staining the floor deep red.

Doctors consult on the merits of his repair,
   but the damage so familiar to me, I know
   they will never find: the nerves that fire anger
   like a repeater rifle, the belly that burns with the rage
   of the sun, the eyes that search for wolves on the prowl
   outside his house of straw. Miles from the hospital,
   I stare at my name on the paper that grants me
   the power of God over his life until words crack
   like river ice, breaking the seal of winter.

WALKING IN A FOG

We share a path. I have greeted him
cheerfully and often, but he plods along
like a yoked ox, eyes downcast, mute.
Old enough to be my father. Looks
like him too in his loose blue jeans and
old-man straw hat with its chin strap.
A man with a stone in his shoe, walking
without grace, staring at his own feet.
If my father were still able to walk, he
would do it just that way, without noticing
that when the sun peers through the trees
it makes a grid for tic-tac-toe on your
shoulders, that when the pine trees whine
their country music into the wind they lean
like singers on a stage. Maybe why I want
to shake this total stranger, who comes here
with who knows what burdens, and yell,
"Heads up. It will be over before you know it."

FOREVER SEVEN

A network of plastic tubes carrying
rivers of fluid in and out of her child's
flesh labor a low, steady hiss. Her
bluish eyelids, trimmed with silken
lashes, appear to rest over an easy
dream. Repaired with such skill it
might not have been severed at all,
an ear peeks with the shyness
of a white lily through honeyed hair.
Not a scratch mars the pale, pink face.
She looks like a new doll on display.
"It's time," they tell us.
Before they slice her 7-year-old body
and take the liver promised
to another little girl, we must leave,
and this one must finish dying.

The unclaimed baggage
of my sister's meth-head daughter,
she turns up like a second chance
and leans into our family guilt
so hard we spoil her with Happy Meals
and Wal-Mart Barbies.
A failed flight through the rear window
of the car-- driven by a friend
and slammed by a junkie driver--
and she sails onto a city street,
a parody of her own artwork,
where, arms outstretched, she springs
toward heaven from a bed
of construction-paper flowers.
Strike two for my sister.
As she vows to get even

with the druggie bitch,
her Gatling-gun voice hyphenates
and rips into our hearts:
"I--want--her--back."
"It's time," we hear again.
The doctors must get on
with their bloody harvest.
Two days have passed
since the Easter Sunday crash.
But the only rising in this room
is a howl bubbling like yeast
in our throats; the only miracle, that
we do not drown in our own tears.

LOVE TAP

She has turned off the spigot
that poured out love, allowed the handle
that set it gushing to rust, watched each
new ring of glittery limestone gird it
into place. Though it no longer haunts
her dreams, she peeks at it from the corner
of a wakeful eye. She is careful. Even spying
on love can be dangerous at her age.

PAPER DOLL

Because I'm thin and smooth and small,
he thinks that I'm a paper doll
and cuts my life out along the dotted lines.

And when he's bored with games and play,
he puts me thoroughly away
in a red-brick box he keeps for little things.

A GAME OF LOVE

Inside our party circle
a 13-year-old spins
a bottle of five-cent Coke.
True as a compass needle
its slender neck finds
magnetic North, and the boy
stands there quivering
on the threshold of a kiss.
East and West, relieved.
South grins back tears
as the one she longs for
leans to stoke the fire
smoldering under her best
friend's poodle skirt,
their Dick and Jane hearts
pounding like a fist at the gate
of a brand-new Magic Kingdom.

NEPTUNE'S REVENGE

He runs his tongue
  around her hem
  the way a drinker --
  before that first sweet gulp –
  licks salt from the rim
  of a margarita.
Gray lips in a snarl,
  bored now with teasing,
  he clamps down hard
  on her tight skirt
  and champs and gnaws
  at its gritty fringe.
Whole buildings
  that yesterday stood
  like giant flashlights
  or skinny golden candles
  stuck in a brown cake
  disappear from the shore.
Neptune has not lashed out
  like this since he whipped
  New Orleans to her watery
  knees and bit into her like
  a vampire starved for blood,
  lapping up musicians
  and poor people
  left behind on the streets.

With stale breath and
  hot throat tickling
  from the mix of poisons
  he has tasted in the fouled
  mouth of his mistress,
  the old Roman hoists his trident,

opens the sky,
and heaves into the wind,
growling:
"The Sea is mine.
She has but one God."

THE WAY THROUGH

the swamp is not a freeway
nor the pine trees
skyscrapers that spawn
other skyscrapers. The birds
neither rock stars nor country
music idols. The dead leaves
not refuse, the air not AC
nor the sun a searchlight.
The squirrels keep busy but have
no schedules that are not seasons.
And I am as easy as a worm
sliding through damp earth away
from the world of squawk and gobble.

MEXICAN PETUNIAS

Every morning of summer they wake up
smiling in a pine-straw bed and stretch
their skinny legs, ballet dancers splendid
in tutus of purple-blue. Every afternoon
helped by a sea breeze cruel enough to add
a merciless thrashing to the daily ritual
of their public striptease, the willowy stalks
shed their clothing like blue tears and stand
naked in the hot sun for the rest of the day.
By moonlight they find not only what they
have lost but more cerulean finery and,
miracle of miracles, prepare to smile again.

LEGACY

Remember how, when they were little girls,
we imagined them perfect adults, their lives
cushioned with money and happiness, a link
we believed in then? How they would marry
perfect men in Camelot weddings who would
adore them as we did? How their children
would grow up at least as beautiful as they,
at least as smart, a little army with our own
good genes, strong enough to breach the gates
of Nobel laureates, presidents? We never
meant to pass on our nightmares, you,
the beautiful bluebird, gathering worms
and cleaning the nest, me in camouflage, flying
head down, focused on a new and better
birdhouse. Our innocence passed fast as
a Japanese train hurrying to board the next
generation, and what we gave them in the end
was a version of what we got ourselves.
It takes a powerful formula to change color
into art, notes into symphonies, words into sonnets.
We didn't know alchemy when they were little girls.

THROWBACK

The professor studies the planes
of her face, registering with surprise
the dusky skin taut as the surface of a drum,
catalogues the high cheekbones angling
from almond-shaped eyes the color
of buffalo grass in spring. Mentally he
changes the eyes to charcoal, straightens
the long, dark hair and makes it darker.
The paleontologist in him cannot resist.
"What tribe do you belong to?" Though
the question rattles her, her expression
remains fixed, spare as a squaw's. She
does not see what he sees: the inscrutable
Iroquois eyes, the Oglala Sioux face dark
as a wooden mask, does not recognize
the ancient grandmothers watching her
in every mirror. But buried beneath
the umber skin and shifting in the silence
of her chiseled bones lies a deeper mystery
only I who know her well perceive:
The Old Ones have also claimed my daughter's soul.

THE JELLY LIP SMOOCHERS

At six my Joan of Arc commands a troop
of first-grade girls. When she declares war
they follow her into battle with the blind
obedience of baby ducks. Racing across the
playground in search of the enemy, they spy
one, a little boy leaning against the water
fountain tying his shoelace. Like killer bees
they swarm, stinging him to the ground with
kisses, then swell up fat as cats after a canary
lunch while he deflates into last week's party
balloon. Afraid his friends will see him crying
the child remains face down until my daughter
guides her warriors on a new quest. Word
of Joan and her band of lip-glossed warriors
spreads among the school kids like the flu.
The boys dub them "The Jelly Lip Smoochers."

Now that first-grader, grown into a take-charge
woman, brushes her husband away like a pesky
fly, insisting she is busy and he is not to bother her
with kisses. The rules of engagement have changed.
The war continues.

VALENTINE'S DAY

I wanted the older boy, the tall one who carried me
to school on winter days when my five-year-old
legs could not walk both miles, to be the one to bid
on the box lunch with the pink crepe-paper skirt and
the red construction-paper hearts, wanted to sit
with him and eat the fried chicken and cherry pie my
mother packed for the raffle at our one-room country
schoolhouse, wanted him to be my sweetheart. But
my father's cousin, a grown-up man with a job, was
high bidder for the shoebox full of food and won the
right to sit beside me to eat it. And I was too young
to understand that women are bought and sold against
their wishes every day, even little girls on Valentine's.

FIRST HOLY COMMUNION

I am number two in the procession
of 8-year-olds in filmy white dresses
and net veils marching to the front
pew of St. Ambrose, hands folded
into steeples, eyes downcast. When
Sister Mary Eustace signals with her
clicker, we approach the altar single
file and stick out our tongues
at Fr. Garrity to receive the body
of Christ for the first time. Sister
has assured us that today is so special
we may ask for anything and it will
be granted, but adds it is best to pray
for sainthood. So I do. I ask to be made
a saint, though I am pining for a bicycle.

Down the aisle I go again, this time
in a cloud of bridal white, fingers tight
on the stem of a thorny red rose, eyes
studying my pumps. I am 19 when I
march into the tuxedoed arms
of matrimonial hell, the proving
ground of a litany of women saints.
Thirty-two years later, having failed
at holiness and in the throes of divorce,
I remember that I could have had a bicycle.

TO MY EX-HUSBAND'S EX-GIRLFRIEND

I knew you had some losers to your name,
and I was not surprised you thought your luck
had changed when he arrived, a vision
of metallic charm: the silver waves of flowing
hair, the eyes like steely summer storms.
I'll bet he whined I left with no good-byes--
the years and years and all he'd done for me--
and then you reached to pat his waiting hand
and felt the finger notch, the naked circle
minus wedding band. You must have thought
him, oh, so smart, his fancy talk, the Ph.D.
If you had known I chained myself to office
desks and typed my heart to solid stone
so he could strut in crimson hood, would you
have felt a woman's sympathy for me?
I heard he promised you a country house,
a stripling mare. How nice! A playmate for
the stud I bought for him. I'm sure your heart
ka-thumped delight and asked itself: "What fool
returns a gem like him? A perfect find!"
The rumor is he rode away alone,
the promised house did not materialize.
I'll bet by now you've grasped the simple truth:
He lies and lies and lies.

POEMS OLD AND NEW

My old poems will never appear in public.
Like the offspring of a thalidomide mom,
they were maimed when they slid out of me.
Never mind the occasional participle that
dangles, the infinitive that's split. These
poems sprout verbs that whine like feral cats,
sentences as meandering as lost drunks under
a full moon, a cascade of obtuse adjectives,
the kind that stick to the promises of politicians.
They strangle the truth like weeds choking grass.
I wonder why I don't burn them.

The new ones I have promised a better life,
perhaps something in black and white, crisp
and well-composed like photographic art,
images so confident they will lift from the page:
a middle finger raised like a monument,
a fist clenched in anger. They will be as clear
as a freshly tuned piano, as bold as a Muslim
without her burka. My new poems will keep
no secrets. They will glitter with novelty
and shiver with righteousness.
And they will be heard.

MURDER MYSTERY

At three in the morning an urgent thought jerks my friend from sleep. Her head, swollen with the night's dreaming, throbs like a full bladder. Silent as the dead she floats to her outdoor office, a metal potter's shed, where she settles like a child in a secret hiding place. Impatient with the computer as it grumbles to life, she finds a pen and writes furiously, bleeding herself like her own sick patient. Out spurts another fragment of novel about a woman from the Deep South on trial for the murder of her father. My friend anguishes over how to kill off the antagonist, a handsome military officer with milky skin smooth as a well-told lie and eyes that emit virtue like a statue of Jesus, a man who removes his daughter's innocence like the child changes the clothing of her doll.

As if she were discussing the weather at a party, my friend announces that her food has no taste, that she can't sleep and spends most of her time in the backyard sanctuary. I picture her there, eyes drooping like a rain-soaked night, body thin as a whisper, sagging under a secret burden as she spears the past with writing implements and spreads paragraphs like summer kudzu. How long, I wonder, will this murder take? My friend is not a young woman. "Finish him off," I want to scream at her. "Carve out his lusting heart with your ballpoint and line his casket with revisions. Speak for the little girls who have no words to trump the fleshy memories of their miserable fathers."

"Can you hear me down there, Grandpa? I know what you did."

MOVING ON

Memories of the Midwest follow me South
like frames unwinding from an old movie reel: ice-
crystal winters and springs shabby with storm debris,
summers too tired to cry over the thirsty willows
and the parched grass. I say good-bye to a child left
wandering in the rubble of a long marriage wrecked
like a train, caress the stone cover that marks the last bed
of my first love. Old friends bury me deep as a past life.
Enemies purge what they can without erasing themselves.

Arteries of fresh color spread from the smooth walls
of my Georgia home. Determined to start with a clean slate,
I attack paint flecks on the hardwood floors
like a scrubwoman scouring blood spatter from a surgery.
Outside, the camellias drop their tomato-red blossoms.
Magnolias explode into snowballs. The garden whispers
that my mouth will taste of wine forever if I will stay,
that a blanket of gardenia white will cover
my Southern grave with the smell of heaven.

I have come here reckless as the wind from air
so cold and dry I begged for every breath. Now
I want for nothing. The marsh-brown earth yields
to me with the grace of an old Southern gentleman.
I could pretend to be young again and mold it into
mud pies. Or brighten my hair and sparkle my nails,
parade my colors like the ancient oleanders that wave
their fiery blossoms through one more summer.

The devil finds me napping in a hammock, swaying
with the sea breeze under the shimmer of the golden
sun. While I dream of living on the blue berries from
the wax myrtles and the red fruit from the bottle brush,
he laughs. He knows the tides will never wash away
the footprint of my past, that even in Paradise
I cannot grow a brand-new soul.

THE LIST

She is five when she prints the list in unsteady letters
that lean to the right like rangy flowers looking for sunlight.
Her parents are so proud that her mother posts it on the fridge
and her father posts it on Facebook. She declares herself first.

AVERY
                    Next is
MIMI
                    her other grandmother.
                    There's a line for
MORK
                    crossed out and corrected to
MARK
                    the name of her grown-up half-brother.
MOM
                    and
DAD
                    follow with the final entry reading:

I LOVE IVERBUTTEE

My name is nowhere. I have not made the list. And I am so hurt
that for weeks I hate the brand-new house behind the gate, hate
the sound of the sea and the grit of the sand, hate every single one
of the thousand miles that separate me from my only grandchild.

NATURE TRAIL

Squirrels police the elevated track meandering
through the coastal swamp in our very planned
community. Like gray knights digging their heels
into horse flesh, they grip the handrails and hang
on, leaping into nearby tree arms an instant before
our feet sweep the air. This is not the El. No one
is hurrying anywhere except to see the alligators
motionless as fossils in the shallow bordering
ditches or to follow the sensuous lilt of the birds as
they flirt shamelessly from secret perches. Thin as
lisps of wind and robust as basketballs, we pass, old
and older, the smell of our morning soap vying
with the saltwater air. As woodpeckers drill
their special trees, we chirp over the noise—
"Good morning." "Have a nice day." "Take care"—
and the trees, gnarled and seasoned as we, ignore
the nuisance. Such a short trail to be alarmed
with three red telephones and so many seats for resting
they merge in the eye with the grazing deer anchored
to the forest floor like brown benches. It is fall,
and the wind pelts us with a storm of dried leaves,
as though we were withered stalks enduring
in a forgotten field. Pine needles, slick as January ice,
bed down on the wooden planks, and a brown boy
glazed in daydreams blasts them with a leaf blower.
Like the copperheads hidden in the piles of brush
and under the gold-leaf rubble of the trees,
Time unravels around us.
Otherwise, we are safe
here in the fractured sunlight.

DISCORD

The wind launches an avalanche of pine needles
onto the wooden path, already spread butter-thick
with spongy leaves from today's rain. Conscious
of my aging bones, how they would not take kindly
to a fall, I move cautiously over the slick boards
treacherous as a macadam highway buried
in January ice. Feeling the weight of our latest discord,
I slog on through the pasty mess, kicking around
wishes that we had met sooner, melded better, made
children who would love us or not, envying the deer
who bound through these woods without fear of falling.

TOO BUSY

Stacks of paper mound your desk and
litter mine. Dust collects on tabletops
and shrubs escape the proper shapes we
pruned them in. Our heavy boots leave
footprints where we goosestep to the thrum
of German marching songs our fathers used
to sing. And SS troops patrol our lives
to guarantee we have no time for making love.

CHANGE OF LIFE

When I overtake the slogging
chores that refuse to retire
even though I did and pursue
what I wanted to be
doing while I was doing
everything but, I gawk
at a blank computer face,
its blasé hum of bits and bytes
and gigs of RAM, until my focus
cuts like steel into the gray screen,
peels away pages of nostalgia
for the nine-to-five lingering
in my subtext. A committed lover,
I stroke it awake and urge it
past resistance until I am
firing words like bricks in a kiln,
approaching a literary Big Bang,
becoming who I dreamed.

PAST DESPAIR

I have grayed all over, ashen offering
to the god of long living. Transparent too,
like a woman lately wrapped in parchment
and baked to brittle. You can tour my insides,
see the surfaces where I scratched my ideas
with a spoon when I was a prisoner of myself
on a hunger strike. The skeletons of loved ones
worn down like used chalk stack in my corners,
and my walls are hung with plaques to past
despair. But note how I have buffed my edges
to a shine, like the good leather of a worn shoe.
No longer can I tighten my daily mask, nor do I
care to. I hang outside my zippers like an old man
who no longer cares a whit--who forgets even that
simple business--sassy as ever, saying what is true.

WAKE-UP CALL

When I wake to the rattle of pans and plates
brain soggy with dreaming, I think my mother
is making breakfast and will call me soon
to get up for school. I think I am a child.
But when I catch the ruffled old woman
yawning in the mirror opposite my bed, I know
it is someone else I love who bangs those cymbals
luring me into day with that old familiar symphony.

SHOOTING DOLPHINS

Minutes before the dinner-dance, I wander
out to the patio to peer at the ocean that etches
the clubhouse lawn and spy a pod of dolphins
threading the water's edge. Circling their dinner,
I suppose, though the sea, black as a chalkboard,
blocks my view. Inert and patient, my own meal
waits inside, and a sudden pang prods me toward it.
But as I turn to leave, the sun spreads its orange net
over the silver swimmers, and gooseflesh cools
my skin. Desperate to store this scene, certain I will
long for such memories in some gloomy season, I
stand there in the fading light, clicking and clicking
through the crystalline lens of my hungry eyes.

SHAMROCK

In the corner
of my kitchen
a shamrock
in a clay pot
stretches its thin arms
toward a window
across the room
reaching for light
its three-fingered hands
opened wide
to receive
this daily communion.
When night comes
or darkness
as on a rainy day
the green fingers
fold in prayer
beseeching the Father
and the Holy Spirit
to honor the luck
of all things Irish
and return, oh
blessed sacrament,
the only sun it knows.

VOYEUR

In the thin morning light
a disk, spoke-framed
like the rays a child draws
around her version of the sun.

The open weave of delicate limbs
fine as the threadlike arms and legs
of a ballerina, manacled
between adjacent longleaf pines.

AGAPE

Thank you for inviting me to join:
your bowling league
your golf group
your Wednesday-night card party
the Sunday-morning choir
your book club
breakfast club
wine tasting and
progressive dinner.
But in order to carry on my love affair
with the human race, I need some privacy.

IV

A DAY OF MY OWN

I crave it like a greedy
child eyeing chocolate.
Waking in the dark, I feel
you glide through the sheets,
hear the clunk of quarters
against the floor as you fill
your pockets by feel. Night
watch over, the house alarm
whimpers at the back door.
It is safe to get out of bed.
I run like a batter with bases
loaded from flush to splash
to perk, sliding into home
on my belly and burrowing
deep into the dugout of covers
now cool as a cave in winter.
Cushioned like a queen among
the extra pillows I have claimed,
I hug myself to myself, daybreak
successor to this entire kingdom
of fluff. When I please, I will
stretch out of here. Maybe when
the sun sneaks under the window
shades. Or maybe I will light
this room myself and read until
my vampire hunger drives me
to the next delicious bite
of this precious time alone.

FRIENDS I'VE NEVER MET

Though they do not know
it, I count a few physicists
among my friends, savoring
the company now and then
of those who tell the stories
of beginnings and endings
in elegant numbers unable
to lie. Also the poets,
the fearless ones who explore
the dark caves of feeling
with nothing more than words
for light. I ask no more of them
than any other friend, that they
trust me with their truest truths.
So when I open their books,
I am grateful to find
flaming arrows aimed
at my white-boned ignorance.

USED BOOKS

I see the signs of someone else.
A reddish splotch obscures a word,
a poem with internal bleed.
I think about a cherry smudge,
a glass of wine tipped carelessly.
I want to ask this visitor --
I'm sure a her; don't ask me why --
if she spilled water at the end
or if her tears have raised those bumps
like an invitation that's been embossed.
And could she help me understand
the meaning of the poet's line,
the "weeping grass," the "marshy flesh"?
If we had tea, I might confess that
words like these that lurk in shadows
yet conspire to make me sad.
Perhaps we'd meet to trade *our* poems
or shop around for more used books.
I'd tell her how it makes me feel,
the crease and split along their spines,
the rotting threads at brittle seams,
the breaking down and wearing thin
as onion skin from being used.

SENSIBLE SHOES

Plantar fasciitis and degenerative disc disease
and whatever other –itis and –ease
have turned me from a lean spike to a short squat.
Some days I can barely walk the distance
between my memories and my dreams
even in these sensible shoes.

SOMETIMES WE ARE ONE

In the brown dawn of a winter day
the deer blend with the trunks of pine trees
and the trees with the brown leaf covering
of the forest floor and the leaves
with the brown earth and the earth
with the wooden path where I meld
with darkness until the sun opens
the roster of day and we are again
deer, trees, leaves, earth, planks, woman.

THE SOUND OF PRAYER

A hum rises in the forest
the buzz of bugs and birds
quivering the boughs
of the thousand pines
anchored to the earth
like a thousand monks
in a cloister choir
who chant their thanks
for the sweetness
of breath, of all that is.

SUNDAY MORNING BEHIND THE GATE

We keep the Sabbath here.
No jackhammers.
No delivery trucks or roof repairs.
If the lawns and shrubs are growing
they have the sense to be quiet about it.
Not even the wind stirs

until a siren rips into Sunday
over a percussion of worried tires
shattering any illusions we harbor
of living forever.

MEN'S EXERCISE CLASS

Tuesdays and Thursdays, 9:00 a.m., they
follow their leader into the Olympic-sized
pool and, more or less in rhythm, bob like
crumbling old corks. Next, water weights,
blue for boy and light as baby rattles, hoisted
half-mast, like children playing at "fitness," a
term shackled for them in permanent quotes.
Only the present exists, even for those once
so godlike their voices sent shivers through
skyscraper floors, whose sense of humor died
a tragic death at the Battle of the Bottom Line.
But also for the not so powerful, the plumbers
and clerks and teachers. With the desperation
of the drowning they thrash side by side, mixed
like garden vegetables in the same watery stew.

SUICIDE IN THE NEIGHBORHOOD

He told his wife he would be at Bob's
then walked deep into the woods, heavy
with summer, where only squirrels and
birds and snakes could see what he was
up to. I don't know why, didn't know him.
A dreaded illness? A nagging sorrow?
Time x'ing out the him that he remembered?
But I know he had had enough, that like
a balloon with a molecule of air too many,
he couldn't hold another drop inside.
His life stretched too tight, he popped.

... WHY THEY CRIED

My grandmother stands on the square
concrete porch of her four-room house.
She wears a print dress cut from a feed sack
under an apron made from a different feed sack.
Above the Cuban heels of her lace-up shoes--
ordered from the Sears catalogue, black,
EEE width--she looks as solid as the porch.
Dressed in his usual long-sleeved gray shirt
and pants, my grandfather bends toward her
as if lending or seeking support. His hair
matches her shoes. Her hair, corralled
in its gray bun, blends with his sleeve.
From the back seat of a 1948 maroon DeSoto,
I wave good-bye, puzzled by the maze of tears
exploring my grandparents' scored cheeks.

With stiff fingers I tow the zipper around a small
pink suitcase sprinkled with miniature elephants,
its metal teeth closing around my granddaughter's
summer visit. That's when I see them, side by side
like bookends on an empty shelf.
That's when I know . . .

I WANT TO BE FIRST

Our limbs twist together like old vines in a dark forest.
Your heavy trunk cushions my head against the black
tangle that flowers there the way moss thrives on bark.
I burrow against the cold and take nourishment from
your mouth like a baby bird learning to live. So lined
with sinew they could be Doric columns, your arms
bend over me in a canopy of striated flesh. Eyes the
color of lonely blue lakes punctuate like neon the sweet
time before we sleep. All day long you watch over me
in our private Eden, clearing the paths I wander, smashing
even twigs that might bruise my toes, trumpeting a warning
to predators and fools. You are my Adam, my Atlas,
my fiery prince. But as my bones dry to chalk and my
Technicolor days fade like autumn yielding to Midwest
winter, a preview of a black-and-white life alone winds like
a pall around my thoughts. While the words lick the edges
of our moments, neither of us reveals that we expect to be
the first to slide the length of our failing knot into oblivion.

MAY

She sneaks up on me every time,
shocks me with her glut of blooming
bulbs and bushes and trees so dazzling
they startle themselves with their new
clothing. Even fish arc out of the water
to have a look at her. Then I remember
how on her sixth day she opened a deep
pocket in the lining of her new green skirt
and tucked my mother away for keeps.
And I want to know: How dare she come
here every spring as if she had nothing
to hide, flaunting that same old beauty?

SWAMP DOE

Motionless as some hunter's
prized mount, a head pokes
through a garland of leaves.
The rest hides in the spongy
quilt of pine needles, twigs,
other leaves warming
the November swamp floor.
A fine daybed, I think, a safe place
to rest until night turns her loose
to look for food and other creatures.
With a turn of the head and a stare
she lets me know that I am neither.
Just passing by, deer friend.
Sweet dreams.

HER WAY TO SAY GOOD-BYE

Days before the end of our summer visit,
when I already pine for another dose
of her 8-year-old silliness, already grieve
for her end-of-day refrain:
"Let's get in bed and cuddle,"
she clobbers me:
"When I am back at school and busy
with my friends, I will forget about you."

I want to strike back that in *my* other life
I dance and write poems, take naps
when I please, but a voice inside
drowns me out: Not enough, it insists,
to spare you that empty place at the table
left by the child of your child, an innocent
who understands all one needs to know
about time: how love moves
into the vault of memory
how the moment surrounds us
like an opaque balloon
how the present collapses
and yesterday steps aside
to make room for tomorrow.

GRANDCHILDREN

They disappear with friends
near age 11. We lose them
to baseball and tennis, garage
bands, slumber parties, stages
where they rehearse for the future,
ripen in a tangle of love knots.
With our artificial knees and hips
we move into the back seats
of their lives, obscure as dust
behind our wrinkles, and sigh
as we add the loss of them
to our growing list of the missing.

Sometimes they come back,
carting memories of sugar cookies
and sandy beaches, memories of how
we sided with them in their wars
with parents, sided with them
even as they slid out of our laps
into the arms of others.

Sometimes they come back
and hold onto our hands
as if they were the thin strings
of helium balloons
about to drift off.

ALL MY WORLDLY GOODS

The day will come when I will leave it all to you:
my few good jewels
the furniture and Jamestown glass
whatever's left of stocks and bonds
my vintage mink and other clothes
(your size if not your taste)
the photo books of births and deaths and fractured lives
and every word I ever wrote and saved.
But not just that:
The earth in its entirety.
Your turn, dear child, to keep or not
and how to use
the whole
beautiful
mad
mess.

ABOUT THE AUTHOR

Olivia was born in Kalispell, Montana, but cradled in the Midwest by a 20-year-old mother, one of 14 children, and a father raw from both the harsh life of a Missouri dirt farm and his stint in the infantry during World War II. She discovered writing in third grade at St. Ambrose Elementary School when her teacher, Sr. Mary Eustace, direct from Ireland, rewrote the paragraph she was assigned with such flare that Olivia tried ever after to emulate her. Her urge to write was cemented when, as a high school senior, she wrote a "fairytale" that sparked so much controversy she was threatened with expulsion.

At 19 she married; at 20, became a mother. A favorite professor hooked her on poetry, but she gave up college to help support her family, and the urge to write went underground. For the next 14 years she worked as a secretary, then as a stenotype reporter--capturing other people's words--for 26 more. At age 52 she divorced her old life, her first husband, longstanding career, and hometown. Olivia remarried and relocated with her current husband, a retired FBI agent, to Bluffton, South Carolina, where they watch birds and alligators and dance the Carolina Shag like nobody's watching. She writes what she likes in her own words.

Books by Dos Madres Press

Mary Margaret Alvarado - *Hey Folly* (2013)

John Anson - *Jose-Maria de Heredia's Les Trophées* (2013)

Jennifer Arin - *Ways We Hold* (2012)

Michael Autrey - *From The Genre Of Silence* (2008)

Paul Bray - *Things Past and Things to Come* (2006), *Terrible Woods* (2008)

Jon Curley - *New Shadows* (2009), *Angles of Incidents* (2012)

Sara Dailey - *Earlier Lives* (2012)

Richard Darabaner - *Plaint* (2012)

Deborah Diemont - *Wanderer* (2009), *Diverting Angels* (2012)

Joseph Donahue - *The Copper Scroll* (2007)

Annie Finch - *Home Birth* (2004)

Norman Finkelstein - *An Assembly* (2004), *Scribe* (2009)

Gerry Grubbs - *Still Life* (2005), *Girls in Bright Dresses Dancing* (2010)

Ruth D. Handel - *Tugboat Warrior* (2013)

Richard Hague - *Burst, Poems Quickly* (2004),
    During The Recent Extinctions (2012)

Pauletta Hansel - *First Person* (2007), *What I Did There* (2011)

Michael Heller - *A Look at the Door with the Hinges Off* (2006),
    Earth and Cave (2006)

Michael Henson - *The Tao of Longing & The Body Geographic* (2010)

R. Nemo Hill - *When Men Bow Down* (2012)

W. Nick Hill - *And We'd Understand Crows Laughing* (2012)

Eric Hoffman - *Life At Braintree* (2008), *The American Eye* (2011),
    By The Hours (2013)

James Hogan - *Rue St. Jacques* (2005)

Keith Holyoak - *My Minotaur* (2010), *Foreigner* (2012)

David M. Katz - *Claims of Home* (2011)

Burt Kimmelman - *There Are Words* (2007), *The Way We Live* (2011)

Pamela L. Laskin - *Plagiarist* (2012)

Richard Luftig - *Off The Map* (2006)

Austin MacRae - *The Organ Builder* (2012)

J. Morris - *The Musician, Approaching Sleep* (2006)

Rick Mullin - *Soutine* (2012)

Robert Murphy - *Not For You Alone* (2004), *Life in the Ordovician* (2007),
    From Behind The Blind (2013)

Pam O'Brien - *The Answer To Each Is The Same* (2012)

Peter O'Leary - *A Mystical Theology of the Limbic Fissure* (2005)

Bea Opengart - *In The Land* (2011)

David A. Petreman - *Candlelight in Quintero - bilingual edition* (2011)

Paul Pines - *Reflections in a Smoking Mirror* (2011)

David Schloss - *Behind the Eyes* (2005)

William Schickel - *What A Woman* (2007)

Lianne Spidel & Anne Loveland - *Pairings* (2012)

Murray Shugars - *Songs My Mother Never Taught Me* (2011),
    Snakebit Kudzu (2013)

Nathan Swartzendruber - *Opaque Projectionist* (2009)

Jean Syed - *Sonnets* (2009)

Madeline Tiger - *The Atheist's Prayer* (2010), *From the Viewing Stand* (2011)

James Tolan - *Red Walls* (2011)

Henry Weinfield - *The Tears of the Muses* (2005),
    Without Mythologies (2008), *A Wandering Aramaean* (2012)

Donald Wellman - *A North Atlantic Wall* (2010),
    The Cranberry Island Series (2012)

Anne Whitehouse - *The Refrain* (2012)

Martin Willetts Jr. - *Secrets No One Must Talk About* (2011)

Tyrone Williams - *Futures, Elections* (2004), *Adventures of Pi* (2011)

www.dosmadres.com